PATRICK H. PERRINE

Master the Money

*Unleashing Financial Acumen for Entrepreneurial
Success*

First edition

ISBN: 9798884865655

*This book was professionally typeset on Reedsy.
Find out more at reedsy.com*

DEDICATION

To the visionary entrepreneurs who dare to dream, innovate, and transform possibilities into reality—this book is dedicated to you. "Master the Money" is a tribute to your courage, resilience, and unwavering determination in the pursuit of greatness. May this guide illuminate your path, empower your decisions, and propel you towards boundless success in the dynamic world of entrepreneurship.

Warmly,
Patrick

"The stock market is filled with individuals who know the price of everything, but the value of nothing."

— PHILIP FISHER

Contents

Preface

Welcome to 'Master the Money: Unleashing Financial Acumen for Entrepreneurial Success,' the next critical step in the 'Be A Unicorn' series, directly expanding on the finance and investment strategies introduced in Step 8 of 'Unicorn Rising.' This volume is not merely a continuation of our exploration into the entrepreneurial journey; it is a practical workbook designed to arm you with the financial knowledge and tools essential for navigating the complexities of business finance.

Understanding the intricacies of finance is crucial for any entrepreneur aiming to steer their venture towards sustainable growth and success. 'Master the Money' serves as your comprehensive guide through this complex landscape, offering deep dives into financial planning, investment strategies, risk management, and beyond. Each chapter is laden with practical exercises, real-world case studies, and actionable advice, ensuring you can apply what you learn directly to your business endeavors.

As part of the 'Be A Unicorn' series, 'Master the Money' reinforces the series' goal to provide a holistic entrepreneurial education. By building upon the insights and strategies from previous volumes, this book ensures a seamless progression in your learning journey, enhancing your financial literacy and strategic thinking.

I encourage you to actively engage with this book, embracing it as a tool for transformation and growth. Through its pages, you'll uncover the secrets to making informed financial decisions, optimizing resources, and ultimately driving your venture's success.

'Master the Money' is your roadmap to mastering the financial aspects of entrepreneurship. By delving into this book, you commit to unlocking the full potential of your entrepreneurial vision, equipped with the financial acumen needed to navigate the challenges and opportunities of the business world.

Prepare to deepen your understanding of finance and investment, as 'Master the Money' guides you through each concept with clarity and precision. Let's embark on this journey together, transforming insights from 'Unicorn Rising' into actionable financial strategies that propel your entrepreneurial dreams into reality.

Are you ready to master the money? Let's dive in and unleash your financial acumen for entrepreneurial success!

Be A Unicorn: The New Entrepreneur's Ultimate Guide To Success

Dream It, Build It:
An Aspirational Odyssey Through
Entrepreneurship in Ten Inspiring Volumes.

Volume Eight

MASTER THE MONEY

Unleashing Financial Acumen for Entrepreneurial Success

1

Financial Planning and Goal Setting

"Plan your work for today and every day,
then work your plan."
– Margaret Thatcher

F inancial planning and goal setting are the bedrocks upon which successful businesses are built. They form the compass that guides entrepreneurs through the often turbulent waters of launching and growing a business. These processes go beyond mere number crunching; they embody the strategic visioning and meticulous execution that turn dreams into reality. This chapter seeks to illuminate the path toward effective financial planning and goal setting, laying out the strategies that ensure a firm's financial health and resilience.

At the heart of financial planning lies the dual focus on creating sustainable growth and safeguarding against potential pitfalls. It involves a comprehensive examination of financial resources, investment strategies, and market opportunities, all while aligning with the broader vision of the company. Goal setting, on the other hand, is the art of translating this vision into actionable, measurable targets. Together, these disciplines enable entrepreneurs to steer their ventures with confidence, navigating challenges and seizing opportunities with precision.

Through real-world examples and actionable insights, this chapter aims to demystify the complexities of financial planning and goal setting. By breaking down the components of a solid financial plan and exploring effective goal-setting techniques, entrepreneurs will be equipped with the tools needed to build a robust foundation for their business ventures. From understanding cash flow dynamics to setting achievable financial milestones, the focus will be on practical strategies that can be applied to ensure long-term success and adaptability in the ever-evolving business landscape.

Opening Anecdote: Spanx's Blueprint: From Concept to Billion-Dollar Brand

Consider the journey of Sarah Blakely, the founder of Spanx. With nothing but an idea and $5,000 in savings, Blakely turned a simple concept into a billion-dollar empire. Her success story underscores the power of precise financial planning and goal setting. Blakely's meticulous approach to budgeting, coupled with her clear vision, propelled Spanx from a one-product wonder to a global brand.

> **Quick Thought:**
> *Financial goals are not just numbers on a spreadsheet; they are the aspirations that fuel our drive to succeed.*

Entrepreneurship in Action: Key Ingredients

- **Vision and Precision:** Knowing where you want your business to go and having a clear, detailed financial roadmap to get there.
- **Adaptability:** Being prepared to pivot and adjust your financial strategies in response to market changes and business growth.
- **Resilience:** The determination to stick to your financial plans and goals, even when faced with setbacks.

Case Study: Warby Parker's Revolutionary Approach to Eyewear

Background: Warby Parker, a pioneering eyewear brand, was founded with a rebellious spirit and a lofty objective: to offer designer eyewear at a revolutionary price, while leading the way for socially conscious businesses. The founders—Neil Blumenthal, Andrew Hunt, David Gilboa, and Jeffrey Raider— were frustrated with the high cost of eyeglasses. They saw an opportunity to radically transform the eyewear industry through innovative financial planning and direct-to-consumer sales.

Approach: The team embarked on a mission to bypass traditional channels, design glasses in-house, and engage with customers directly through their website and retail stores. This strategy drastically cut the costs associated with middlemen and retail space, allowing Warby Parker to offer high-quality, stylish eyewear at a fraction of the usual price. They also implemented a Home Try-On program, where customers could order five pairs of glasses to try on at home for free, further personalizing the shopping experience and reducing financial risks for the buyer.

Solution: Warby Parker's customer-centric business model and innovative use of technology disrupted the traditional eyewear market. They used their savings from the direct-to-consumer approach to fund the production of high-quality eyewear and invested in social entrepreneurship, promising to donate a pair of glasses for every pair sold.

Impact: Warby Parker's impact on the eyewear industry has been profound. They've not only offered an affordable alternative to designer eyewear but have also set new standards for corporate responsibility and customer service. Their success has inspired a wave of direct-to-consumer companies across various industries, demonstrating the power of disruptive financial planning and goal setting in entrepreneurship.

Legacy and Insights: Warby Parker's journey is a testament to the importance of innovative financial planning, goal setting, and a customer-first approach in building a successful business. Their strategy of cutting out the middleman, offering exceptional value, and committing to social responsibility has not only led to substantial financial success but has also established a new paradigm in the eyewear industry.

Pro Tip: Always align your financial goals with your business's core values and long-term vision. This alignment ensures that every financial decision propels you closer to your overarching objectives.

Exercise: Financial Mastery Exploration

1. Goal Setting for Financial Clarity:

- **Identify Your Financial Baseline:** Review your current financial statements to understand your starting point. Note your revenue, costs, and profit margins.
- **Define Clear Financial Goals:** Utilizing the SMART criteria, set specific, measurable, achievable, relevant, and time-bound financial goals for your business.
- **Prioritize Your Goals:** Rank your financial goals in order of importance and feasibility. Consider the impact of each goal on your overall business strategy.

2. Strategic Planning for Financial Growth:

- **Develop Action Plans:** For each top-priority goal, outline the steps needed to achieve it. Include resources required, timelines, and responsible parties.
- **Assess Risks and Contingencies:** Identify potential risks to achieving your financial goals and develop contingency plans to address these risks.
- **Schedule Regular Reviews:** Set a schedule for regular review of your financial goals and progress. Adjust your action plans based on performance and external changes.

3. Financial Analysis and Adjustment:

- **Perform Financial Ratio Analysis:** Use financial ratios to analyze your company's performance. Focus on liquidity ratios, profitability ratios, and efficiency ratios.

- **Adjust Budgets Based on Analysis:** Based on your financial analysis, make necessary adjustments to your budgets to align with your financial goals.
- **Innovate and Iterate:** Continuously look for innovative ways to improve financial performance. Be open to iterating on your strategies based on what the financial data tells you.

Challenge For You: Select one aspect of your business's financial planning that you've previously overlooked or avoided. It could be detailed cash flow analysis, forecasting, or setting up a contingency fund. Tackle this challenge head-on, applying the principles outlined in this chapter to create a plan of action. How does addressing this challenge change your perspective on financial planning and goal setting?

Conclusion: The journey of financial planning and goal setting is both challenging and rewarding. As entrepreneurs, mastering these skills is crucial for navigating the complex world of business finance. By setting clear financial goals and developing a comprehensive plan to achieve them, you position your business for sustainable growth and success. Remember, the goal is not just to survive but to thrive. Let the stories and strategies shared in this chapter serve as your guide as you embark on your financial planning journey.

2

Budgeting and Cost Management

"Budgeting isn't about limiting yourself—
it's about making the things that excite you possible."
– Elizabeth Warren

I n the entrepreneurial world, mastering the disciplines of budgeting and cost management is akin to charting a course through uncharted waters. These financial tools are not just about keeping track of numbers; they are strategic implements in an entrepreneur's arsenal, designed to optimize resources, drive growth, and secure the longevity of their venture. This chapter ventures deep into the core of budgeting and cost management, illuminating their pivotal role in maintaining financial health and propelling business success.

At the heart of effective financial management lies the dual imperative of meticulous planning and vigilant cost control. Budgeting serves as the blueprint of a business's financial strategy, laying out a detailed map of expected income, expenditures, and financial goals. It is a dynamic process, requiring regular adjustments and refinements to adapt to the ever-evolving business landscape. Cost management, on the other hand, focuses on maximizing the value of every dollar spent, ensuring that the business operates efficiently without compromising the quality of its offerings or its competitive edge.

Together, budgeting and cost management form the foundation upon which sustainable businesses are built. They enable entrepreneurs to forecast financial challenges, identify opportunities for savings, and make informed decisions that bolster growth. Through real-world anecdotes, insightful case studies, and practical exercises, this chapter aims to equip entrepreneurs with the knowledge and tools needed to navigate the complex terrain of financial planning and cost management, transforming these tasks from necessary evils into powerful strategies for success.

Opening Anecdote: Ring's Budgeting Brilliance: Paving the Way from Garage to Amazon

Jamie Siminoff's journey with Ring, a home security company, illustrates the transformative power of meticulous budgeting and strategic cost management. Starting in his garage with limited funds, Siminoff was forced to make every dollar count. Through careful budgeting and a focus on cost-effective marketing strategies, Ring was able to grow from a garage project to a company acquired by Amazon for over $1 billion. This story is a testament to how effective financial management can turn limitations into opportunities.

Quick Thought:

Effective budgeting and cost management transform financial constraints into strategic advantages.

Entrepreneurship in Action: Key Ingredients

- **Precision Planning:** Detailed and realistic budgeting aligns your financial resources with your business goals, ensuring every dollar serves a purpose.
- **Cost Awareness:** A deep understanding of your cost structure enables you to identify savings without sacrificing quality.
- **Adaptive Management:** Regularly reviewing and adjusting your budget and costs in response to business dynamics keeps your financial strategy agile and effective.

Case Study: Case Study: TOMS Shoes - A Model of Social Entrepreneurship and Financial Acumen

Background: TOMS Shoes, founded by Blake Mycoskie, pioneered a unique business model that blended social responsibility with profitability. Starting with the simple idea of giving a pair of shoes to a child in need for every pair sold, TOMS faced the challenge of managing costs while fulfilling its mission.

Approach: TOMS implemented a dynamic budgeting approach, carefully balancing costs with its philanthropic goals. The company focused on direct-to-consumer sales channels and leveraged social media for marketing, significantly reducing costs compared to traditional retail and advertising methods.

Solution: By prioritizing cost-effective supply chain solutions and creating a strong brand that encouraged customer loyalty, TOMS was able to maintain a sustainable business model. Their budgeting practices allowed them to manage the cost of donations within their overall financial plan, ensuring the company's growth and ability to continue its mission.

Impact: TOMS Shoes has donated over 96 million pairs of shoes to children in need, demonstrating that strategic budgeting and cost management can coexist with a powerful social mission. Their success has inspired a new generation of entrepreneurs to consider how business can be a force for good.

Legacy and Insights: The story of TOMS Shoes highlights the importance of innovative budgeting and cost management in supporting both profitability and social impact. It showcases how entrepreneurs can use financial tools to balance business objectives with ethical considerations.

Pro Tip: Leverage technology to streamline your budgeting and cost management processes. Tools like cloud-based accounting software and budgeting apps can provide real-time insights into your financial performance, automate tedious tasks, and enable more accurate forecasting. Embracing these technologies not only saves time but also enhances decision-making with up-to-date financial data.

Exercise: Budgeting Workshop

1. Budgeting Mastery:

- **Craft Your Budget:** Develop a detailed budget for your next quarter. Include all expected revenues, fixed costs, and variable expenses.
- **Scenario Planning:** Create three financial scenarios (best case, worst case, and most likely) to understand potential financial outcomes and prepare accordingly.
- **Budget Review Ritual:** Schedule monthly budget reviews to compare actuals against projections, identify variances, and adjust future budgets based on learnings.

2. Cost Management Deep Dive:

- **Cost Identification:** List all your major cost categories. For each, identify whether it's fixed, variable, or semi-variable.
- **Cost Reduction Brainstorm:** For each major cost category, brainstorm at least three strategies for reducing costs without compromising product or service quality.
- **Implement and Track:** Choose one cost reduction strategy to implement in the next month. Track its impact on your budget and evaluate its effectiveness.

3. Strategic Financial Decisions:

- **Investment Analysis:** Identify one area in your business where investing more could lead to greater returns. Analyze the potential benefits and costs.

- **Break-Even Analysis:** Conduct a break-even analysis for a new product or service you're considering. Use this to inform pricing and marketing strategies.
- **Long-Term Planning:** Outline a long-term financial plan that includes growth projections, investment needs, and strategic financial goals.

Challenge For You:

Take a closer look at an area of your business where budgeting and cost management have been challenging. Using the exercises above, develop a comprehensive plan to address these challenges. Reflect on how a structured financial approach can not only solve immediate issues but also lay the groundwork for sustained financial health and strategic growth.

Conclusion:

This chapter underscores the indispensable role of budgeting and cost management in crafting a successful entrepreneurial narrative. By integrating these financial disciplines into your daily operations, you pave the way for informed decision-making, efficient resource allocation, and ultimately, the achievement of your business aspirations. Let the principles and practices shared here guide you toward financial mastery and business excellence.

3

Financial Statements and Analysis

"Numbers have an important story to tell.
They rely on you to give them a voice."
– Stephen Few

N avigating the financial landscape of a business requires more than just intuition; it necessitates a firm grasp of financial statements and the stories they tell about a company's past, present, and potential future. For entrepreneurs, these documents are not mere formalities but are the lifeblood of business strategy, offering insights that inform every critical decision. This chapter aims to demystify financial statements, breaking down their components and demonstrating how to wield them as powerful tools for analysis and strategic planning.

Understanding the intricacies of financial statements can transform them from intimidating reports into illuminating narratives of a business's financial journey. Whether it's identifying trends in revenue and expenses, assessing financial health, or planning for future growth, these documents hold the key to informed decision-making. Through a deeper exploration of their purpose, components, and the strategic insights they offer, entrepreneurs can unlock new levels of financial literacy and business acumen.

The journey through financial analysis is not just about numbers; it's about understanding the economic forces and operational decisions that drive those numbers. As we delve into the world of financial statements, we'll explore how they reflect the outcomes of strategic choices and operational efficiencies, and how they can be used to steer a business towards its goals.

Opening Anecdote: Nasty Gal's Financial Insight: The Catalyst for Fashion Retail Success

Sophia Amoruso's journey with Nasty Gal from a small eBay store to a fashion retail giant is a testament to the power of financial statement analysis. With keen attention to her business's financial statements, Amoruso was able to pinpoint which fashion lines were most profitable, understand her cost structures, and identify growth opportunities. This analytical approach enabled her to strategically scale Nasty Gal, proving that financial literacy is a cornerstone of entrepreneurial success.

Quick Thought:
Financial statements are not just numbers; they are narratives that, when understood, can guide a business to thrive in the most challenging environments.

Entrepreneurship in Action: Key Ingredients

- **Financial Literacy:** Mastery over the language of financial statements opens doors to deeper insights and more confident decision-making.
- **Analytical Mindset:** The ability to dissect and interpret financial data uncovers the underlying health and potential of a business.
- **Strategic Application:** Leveraging financial insights for strategic planning ensures that business decisions are data-driven and aligned with long-term goals.

Case Study: Beyond Meat - A Financial Growth Story

Background: Beyond Meat, a leader in plant-based meat products, offers a compelling case study on the strategic use of financial statements to fuel rapid growth and market penetration. Founded by Ethan Brown in 2009, the company navigated through the complexities of the food industry by making informed decisions grounded in financial analysis.

Approach: Beyond Meat's management regularly analyzed their income statements to understand revenue trends and cost of goods sold (COGS), identifying opportunities to improve margins by optimizing production processes. Their balance sheet analysis focused on managing inventory efficiently and using assets to support expansion. Cash flow statements were pivotal in ensuring that the company maintained sufficient liquidity to fund R&D and market expansion, especially in the early growth stages.

Solution: Armed with insights from their financial statements, Beyond Meat strategically invested in technology and marketing, improving product offerings and expanding their footprint. This approach not only enhanced their profitability but also positioned them as a strong competitor in the global market.

Impact: The strategic use of financial analysis has been crucial in Beyond Meat's journey to becoming a publicly-traded company with a multi-billion dollar valuation. Their ability to translate financial data into actionable strategies has led to significant growth, increased market share, and a strong financial position in the competitive landscape of the food industry.

Legacy and Insights: Beyond Meat's story underscores the importance of financial statements and analysis in guiding strategic decisions. It highlights how understanding financial nuances can drive operational improvements, strategic investments, and sustainable growth.

Pro Tip: Incorporate financial statement analysis into your regular business review process. This ongoing attention to financial detail will help you stay aligned with your business goals and adapt to changes more swiftly.

Exercise: Mastering Financial Analysis

1. Understanding Your Financial Statements:

- **Income Statement Review:** Identify your main revenue sources and categorize your expenses. Calculate key profitability metrics.

- **Balance Sheet Examination:** Analyze your assets, liabilities, and equity to assess the financial stability and liquidity of your business.
- **Cash Flow Scrutiny:** Understand how cash moves through your business and identify areas to improve cash management.

2. Trend and Ratio Analysis:

- **Perform Trend Analysis:** Compare financial data over several periods to identify patterns, growth trends, or concerning fluctuations.
- **Conduct Ratio Analysis:** Calculate liquidity, solvency, and profitability ratios to evaluate the financial health of your business.

3. Strategic Financial Decisions:

- **Leverage Financial Insights:** Use your analysis to make informed strategic decisions, such as investing in growth opportunities or cutting costs.
- **Plan for the Future:** Develop financial forecasts based on your historical analysis to guide your business strategy moving forward.

Challenge For You:

Choose an area of your financial statements that you find challenging or have neglected. Apply the detailed exercises above, focusing on that area. Reflect on how this analysis changes your understanding of your business's financial health and informs your strategic decisions.

Conclusion:

Financial statements are a goldmine of insights for entrepreneurs willing to dig into the details. Beyond Meat's journey exemplifies how strategic financial analysis can illuminate the path to growth and market leadership. As you become more adept at interpreting these financial narratives, you'll find yourself making more informed, confident decisions that drive your business forward.

4

Cash Flow Management and Forecasting

"A penny saved is a penny earned."
– Benjamin Franklin

C ash flow management is the heartbeat of every business, dictating its viability and resilience in the face of financial uncertainties. For entrepreneurs, mastering cash flow is not just about keeping the business afloat; it's about strategically steering the company towards sustainable growth and profitability. In this chapter, we delve into the critical role of cash flow management and forecasting, providing a roadmap for entrepreneurs to navigate their business's financial currents with confidence.

Understanding and optimizing the flow of cash through your business can mean the difference between survival and failure. Effective cash flow management allows businesses to meet their obligations on time, plan for future investments, and avoid unnecessary debt. By examining the components of cash flow, including inflows, outflows, and working capital, entrepreneurs can gain a clearer understanding of their business's financial health and take proactive steps to improve it.

Forecasting future cash flows is equally important, enabling businesses to anticipate and prepare for potential shortfalls or identify opportunities for investment. This foresight is crucial for maintaining liquidity, ensuring operational continuity, and supporting strategic decision-making. Through practical strategies and real-world examples, this chapter aims to equip entrepreneurs with the tools needed to master cash flow management and forecasting, laying the foundation for financial success.

Opening Anecdote: Airbnb's Creative Cash Flow Solutions During Economic Crisis

In the midst of the 2008 financial crisis, Brian Chesky and his co-founders faced a daunting challenge: financing their startup, Airbnb, in an environment where cash was king and trust in economic stability was low. Their innovative solution to cash flow challenges was as unconventional as their business model— selling themed breakfast cereals to fund their operations. This creative approach to generating cash inflow not only kept their startup afloat during critical early stages but also demonstrated the importance of adaptability and innovative thinking in cash flow management. Chesky's ability to think outside the box in managing Airbnb's cash flow laid the groundwork for what would become a global hospitality behemoth, illustrating that effective cash flow management can indeed turn crisis into opportunity.

Quick Thought:
Effective cash flow management transforms financial challenges into opportunities for growth and innovation.

Entrepreneurship in Action: Key Ingredients

- **Vigilant Monitoring:** Keeping a close eye on cash inflows and outflows to ensure financial stability.
- **Strategic Forecasting:** Anticipating future cash needs to make informed business decisions.
- **Proactive Planning:** Using insights from cash flow analysis to optimize operations and fuel growth.

Case Study: Dropbox's Strategic Cash Flow Management

Background: Dropbox, founded by Drew Houston, faced significant cash flow challenges in its early stages. The company needed to manage its cash wisely to fund operations, invest in growth, and scale its technology infrastructure.

Approach: Dropbox implemented rigorous cash flow management practices, closely monitoring its operating expenses and capital investments. The company focused on converting free users to paid subscriptions, a direct inflow that significantly improved its cash position. Additionally, Dropbox optimized its cloud storage costs and streamlined operations to reduce outflows.

Solution: Through careful management and forecasting of cash flow, Dropbox was able to sustain its rapid growth and expand its user base without compromising on service quality. The strategic allocation of resources towards customer acquisition and retention played a critical role in their financial strategy.

Impact: Dropbox's focus on cash flow management not only facilitated its growth but also attracted significant venture capital investment, leading to its successful IPO. The company's ability to maintain healthy cash flow despite aggressive expansion is a testament to the power of strategic financial planning.

```
Pro Tip: Regularly review and adjust your cash flow
forecasts based on actual performance and changing
market conditions. This dynamic approach allows you
to remain flexible and responsive to your business's
financial needs.
```

Exercise: Navigating Your Cash Flow

1. Understanding Cash Flow Dynamics:

- **Track Monthly Cash Flow:** For the next three months, meticulously record all cash inflows and outflows. This will help you grasp the rhythm of your business's cash cycle.
- **Identify Variable vs. Fixed Expenses:** Categorize your expenses into fixed and variable. Understanding which costs fluctuate with business activity can help you manage cash flow more effectively.
- **Analyze Inflow Sources:** Break down your cash inflows by source (sales, financing, investments) to identify which

areas are your strongest contributors and which may need bolstering.

2. Forecasting and Planning:

- **Create a 12-Month Cash Flow Forecast:** Using historical data and future projections, map out your expected cash flow for the next year. Highlight any anticipated cash shortfalls or surpluses.
- **Scenario Planning:** Develop scenarios for best, worst, and most likely financial outcomes. This will prepare you for a range of possibilities and help you plan accordingly.
- **Develop a Contingency Plan:** Based on your scenario planning, create a contingency plan for managing cash flow in adverse conditions. This could involve securing a line of credit, cutting non-essential expenses, or other liquidity-preserving measures.

3. Optimization Strategies:

- **Improve Receivables:** Implement strategies to accelerate cash inflows, such as offering discounts for early payment or tightening credit terms for customers.
- **Streamline Payables:** Review your payables process to find opportunities to extend payment terms or consolidate supplier payments, ensuring you maintain good supplier relationships while optimizing cash outflows.
- **Regular Cash Flow Reviews:** Establish a routine for regular review of your cash flow statement. This ongoing process will help you stay ahead of potential issues and adjust your strategies as your business evolves.

Challenge For You:

Select an area from the exercises above that represents a new or challenging aspect of cash flow management for you. Focus on implementing these exercises in that area over the next quarter. Reflect on how this focused effort enhances your understanding and management of cash flow, and consider how you can apply these lessons to other financial aspects of your business.

Conclusion:

Cash flow management and forecasting are indispensable tools for any entrepreneur. They provide the clarity needed to navigate financial uncertainties, plan for future growth, and ensure the business's longevity. By mastering these financial disciplines, entrepreneurs can position their businesses for success in the competitive marketplace. The journey of Dropbox showcases how effective cash flow management can support business scalability and financial health, underscoring the importance of this skill for all entrepreneurs.

5

Funding Strategies and Sources

"Money is like gasoline during a road trip. You don't want to run out of gas on your trip, but you're not doing a tour of gas stations."
– Tim O'Reilly

F unding isn't just the fuel that powers the entrepreneurial engine; it's the critical resource that transforms vision into reality. This chapter delves into the multifaceted world of funding, examining why it's indispensable for entrepreneurs, exploring diverse strategies to secure it, and navigating the plethora of sources available.

The quest for funding is a journey every entrepreneur must embark on, whether at the inception of their venture or as part of a strategic move to catalyze growth. The ability to secure adequate funding not only kickstarts operations but also empowers businesses to scale, innovate, and navigate the inevitable ebbs and flows of cash flow management. This chapter aims to illuminate the path to securing funding, outlining strategic approaches and demystifying the sources of capital available to today's entrepreneurs.

Beyond the mechanics of acquiring funds lies the significance of choosing the right mix of funding sources—a decision that can shape the trajectory of a business. From maintaining control over your startup by bootstrapping to leveraging external financing for accelerated growth, the strategy you choose must align with your business goals, values, and vision for the future.

Navigating the funding landscape requires a blend of strategic foresight, financial acumen, and an unwavering commitment to your business's core mission. As we explore the avenues for funding, remember that each choice carries its own set of implications for the future of your venture.

Opening Anecdote: LinkedIn's Calculated Growth: The Art of Strategic Funding

Reid Hoffman's journey with LinkedIn exemplifies strategic funding at its finest. In its early days, LinkedIn faced the challenge of scaling a professional network amidst fierce competition. Hoffman's approach to funding was as innovative as his vision for the platform: he combined personal investments with strategic angel funding to kickstart operations, meticulously avoiding over-reliance on external capital to retain control and flexibility. This judicious approach to funding not only allowed LinkedIn to grow organically but also positioned it attractively for subsequent rounds of venture capital, ultimately leading to one of the most successful tech IPOs of its time. Hoffman's story highlights the importance of a balanced funding strategy that supports growth while preserving the founder's vision and control.

> **Quick Thought:**
> *Selecting a funding strategy is as critical as the business model itself; the right choice can propel a venture to success, while the wrong one can steer it off course.*

Entrepreneurship in Action: Key Ingredients

- **Strategic Vision:** Understanding the long-term implications of different funding sources on your business.
- **Financial Savvy:** Navigating the complexities of funding options with a keen eye on terms, conditions, and potential equity dilution.
- **Relationship Building:** Cultivating networks with potential investors, partners, and financial institutions as a cornerstone of fundraising efforts.

Case Study: Canva's Funding Journey

Background: Canva, an Australian graphic design platform, was co-founded by Melanie Perkins, Cliff Obrecht, and Cameron Adams. The initial concept was born from Perkins' observation of the complexity of traditional design tools and her desire to simplify graphic design for everyone. Despite its potential, turning this vision into a globally successful platform required significant funding.

Approach: Canva's funding journey began with seed funding from angel investors, including Lars Rasmussen, co-founder of Google Maps. This early support was crucial for developing the platform's prototype and gaining user traction. However, to scale their operations globally, the Canva team needed more substantial financial backing.

Solution: The company opted for a mix of equity financing and venture capital to fuel its growth. Over several funding rounds, Canva attracted investments from notable venture capital firms, including Felicis Ventures, Blackbird Ventures, and Sequoia Capital. This influx of capital enabled Canva to expand its product offerings, enter new markets, and continuously enhance its platform.

Impact: Canva's strategic approach to funding has been instrumental in its rise to a multi-billion dollar valuation. By securing funding from investors who also provided mentorship and industry connections, Canva was able to accelerate its growth, expand its user base to millions worldwide, and establish itself as a leading design platform.

Legacy and Insights: Canva's funding journey highlights the importance of choosing the right funding strategy and sources. The company's ability to leverage its funding for global expansion while maintaining its mission to democratize design showcases the power of strategic investment in realizing entrepreneurial visions.

```
Pro Tip: Before seeking external funding, develop a
clear, compelling narrative about your business's
value proposition, growth potential, and how the
funds will be used. This story is crucial for
attracting the right investors and securing favorable
terms.
```

Exercise: Crafting Your Funding Strategy

1. Assess Your Funding Needs:

- **Quantify Your Funding Requirements:** Break down the capital needed for each aspect of your business, from initial setup to operational costs and expansion plans.
- **Prioritize Your Funding Goals:** Determine which areas of your business require immediate funding and which can be phased over time.

2. Explore Funding Sources:

- **Research Available Options:** Compile a list of potential funding sources that align with your business type, industry, and growth stage.
- **Evaluate the Pros and Cons:** Assess each option's implications for equity, control, and future financial obligations.

3. Prepare for Fundraising:

- **Develop Your Pitch:** Create a compelling pitch deck that succinctly outlines your business model, market opportunity, competitive advantage, and financial projections.
- **Network and Build Relationships:** Identify and engage with potential investors or financial institutions through networking events, industry conferences, and direct outreach.

Challenge For You:

Identify one funding source that you previously considered

out of reach or misaligned with your business model. Research this source thoroughly, understanding its requirements, benefits, and drawbacks. Prepare a hypothetical pitch tailored to this funding source, reflecting on how this exercise expands your perspective on funding opportunities and strategic planning.

Conclusion:

Securing funding is a pivotal step in an entrepreneur's journey, offering the means to bring visionary ideas to life and sustain business growth. As demonstrated by Reid Hoffman's approach with LinkedIn, a strategic and balanced approach to funding can significantly impact a company's trajectory. By carefully selecting and pursuing funding sources that align with your business goals and values, you can lay a solid foundation for success. As we move forward, the upcoming chapters will delve deeper into financial modeling, investment strategies, and navigating the financial decisions that shape the future of your venture.

6

Financial Risk Management

"Risk comes from not knowing what you're doing."
– Warren Buffett

I n the entrepreneurial journey, navigating financial risks is akin to sailing in unpredictable waters. Understanding these risks and preparing strategies to manage them is not just about avoiding losses; it's about charting a course for sustained growth and stability. This chapter unpacks the essence of financial risk management, shedding light on its importance, types of financial risks, and effective strategies to mitigate them, ensuring entrepreneurs are well-equipped to protect their ventures.

Financial risk looms as a constant challenge for entrepreneurs, where a single oversight can lead to significant financial distress. Recognizing and managing financial risk is paramount, as it directly impacts a business's ability to generate profit, maintain cash flow, and achieve long-term financial stability. By adopting a proactive approach to financial risk management, entrepreneurs can shield their businesses from potential financial pitfalls, ensuring they remain resilient in the face of economic uncertainties.

Financial risks can arise from a myriad of sources, including market dynamics, credit dependencies, operational hiccups, and liquidity constraints. Identifying these risks early and understanding their potential impact on the business is the first step towards effective risk management. This chapter aims to arm entrepreneurs with the knowledge and tools needed to navigate the complex landscape of financial risk, fostering a robust foundation for their business's financial health.

At the heart of financial risk management lies the capacity to make informed decisions. By integrating risk assessment into strategic planning, entrepreneurs can not only mitigate potential losses but also uncover opportunities for growth. It's about turning challenges into stepping stones, using risk management as a strategic tool to enhance business performance and investor confidence.

Opening Anecdote: Salesforce's Risk Management Strategy: Securing the Cloud's Future

Marc Benioff's journey with Salesforce showcases a masterclass in managing operational risk. In the early days, Salesforce faced significant operational challenges, from system downtimes to security concerns, threatening the company's reputation and customer trust. Benioff's strategic decision to prioritize and invest heavily in cloud infrastructure and security measures not only mitigated these risks but also positioned Salesforce as a reliable and innovative leader in the CRM space. This proactive approach to operational risk management was instrumental in Salesforce's ascent to becoming a cloud computing giant, illustrating the power of foresight and investment in mitigating financial risks.

> ### Quick Thought:
> *Effective financial risk management transforms potential threats into avenues for strategic fortification and innovation.*

Entrepreneurship in Action: Key Ingredients

- **Proactive Identification:** Vigilance in identifying potential financial risks before they materialize.
- **Strategic Diversification:** Employing diversification to spread risk across various revenue streams and investments.
- **Adaptive Planning:** Flexibility in adapting plans and strategies in response to evolving financial risk landscapes.

Case Study: Zara's Market Risk Management

Background: Zara, a flagship brand of the Inditex Group, is renowned for its fast-fashion business model. However, operating in the global market exposes Zara to significant market risks, including currency fluctuations and changing consumer preferences.

Approach: To mitigate these risks, Zara developed a highly responsive supply chain, enabling rapid response to market trends and minimizing inventory risks. Additionally, Zara uses financial instruments to hedge against currency risk, protecting its profit margins from currency fluctuations.

Solution: Zara's agile supply chain and strategic use of financial hedging have allowed it to manage market risks effectively. This approach not only ensures operational efficiency but also maintains Zara's competitive edge in the fast-paced fashion industry.

Impact: Zara's success in managing market risks supports its global expansion and sustains its reputation as a leader in fast fashion. The company's risk management strategies have become a benchmark for the industry, demonstrating how proactive risk management can be a source of strategic advantage.

Pro Tip: Regularly review and update your risk management strategies to reflect changes in your business environment and operations. Staying agile allows you to respond effectively to new risks as they arise.

Exercise: Building Your Risk Management Framework

1. Risk Identification and Assessment:

- **Conduct a Risk Audit:** List all potential financial risks your business might face, including market, credit, operational, and liquidity risks.
- **Evaluate Risk Impact:** Assess the potential impact of each identified risk on your business's financial health and operations.
- **Prioritize Risks:** Rank the risks based on their likelihood

and impact, focusing your management efforts on the most critical risks.

2. Developing Mitigation Strategies:

- **Explore Hedging Options:** Investigate financial instruments or contracts that could hedge against specific risks, such as currency or commodity price fluctuations.
- **Implement Operational Safeguards:** Develop internal controls and processes to minimize operational risks, including robust cybersecurity measures and supply chain diversification.
- **Establish Contingency Funds:** Set aside funds to cover unexpected financial shortfalls, ensuring liquidity during adverse conditions.

3. Monitoring and Review:

- **Set Up a Monitoring System:** Implement a system for regular monitoring of risk indicators and triggers.
- **Review and Adjust Strategies:** Periodically review risk management strategies and adjust them based on new information or changes in the business environment.
- **Educate Your Team:** Ensure that your team is aware of potential financial risks and understands their role in the risk management process.

Challenge For You:
Identify a financial risk your business has not yet encountered but is likely to face in the future. Utilize the exercises above to develop a comprehensive plan to address this potential risk.

Reflect on how preparing for this risk enhances your overall risk management strategy and prepares your business for future challenges.

Conclusion:

Navigating financial risk is an integral part of the entrepreneurial journey. By understanding the types of financial risks and implementing effective strategies to manage them, entrepreneurs can safeguard their business's financial stability and foster sustainable growth. The examples of Salesforce and Zara illustrate the importance of proactive risk management in maintaining a competitive edge and achieving business success. As we move forward, the subsequent chapters will delve deeper into advanced financial management techniques, further equipping entrepreneurs with the skills needed to thrive in the ever-evolving business landscape.

7

Investment Strategies and Capital Allocation

"The wise young man or wage earner of today invests his money in real estate."
– Andrew Carnegie

Embarking on the entrepreneurial journey necessitates not just a vision but the acumen to allocate capital wisely and invest strategically. This chapter delves into the art and science of investment strategies and capital allocation, guiding entrepreneurs through the complexities of maximizing returns, managing risks, and ensuring capital efficiency. Understanding these principles is pivotal for entrepreneurs aiming to nurture growth, build sustainable businesses, and create lasting value.

Investment strategies form the cornerstone of entrepreneurial financial management, influencing how capital is channeled into operations, growth initiatives, and external opportunities. These strategies are multifaceted, tailored to align with business objectives, risk tolerance, and market dynamics. Effective capital allocation, on the other hand, is about precision—ensuring every dollar invested works towards achieving strategic goals, whether it's scaling operations, entering new markets, or innovating product offerings.

The essence of mastering investment strategies lies in the balance between risk and return. Entrepreneurs must navigate this balance, making decisions that propel their businesses forward while safeguarding financial stability. This chapter aims to equip entrepreneurs with the knowledge to craft investment strategies that resonate with their business vision and the practical know-how to allocate capital efficiently, fostering a robust foundation for financial success.

The choice of investment strategy and the technique of capital allocation can significantly impact a business's trajectory. Entrepreneurs face the challenge of identifying opportunities that promise growth and returns in a landscape marked by competition and uncertainty. By adopting a strategic approach to investments and capital allocation, entrepreneurs can unlock new avenues for growth, ensuring their businesses not only survive but thrive in the evolving market landscape.

Opening Anecdote: Starbucks' Expansion Brew: Strategic Investments Stirring Global Success

Howard Schultz's transformation of Starbucks from a local coffee shop into a global phenomenon is a testament to strategic investment and capital allocation. Schultz recognized the potential of Starbucks early on and invested in buying the company, then strategically allocated capital to expand its footprint worldwide. His vision extended beyond mere expansion; Schultz invested in the customer experience, employee training, and product innovation, aspects that became core to Starbucks' identity. This holistic approach to investment and capital allocation was pivotal in Starbucks' journey to becoming a household name, demonstrating the impact of visionary investment strategies on a company's success.

> **Quick Thought:**
> *Strategic investment and prudent capital allocation are the twin engines that drive a business towards its zenith, navigating through the ebbs and flows of market dynamics.*

Entrepreneurship in Action: Key Ingredients

- **Strategic Vision:** Aligning investment strategies with the long-term vision and goals of the business.
- **Risk Assessment:** Judiciously evaluating risks and potential returns to make informed investment decisions.
- **Agile Allocation:** Remaining flexible in capital allocation to seize opportunities and mitigate challenges as they arise.

Case Study: Airbnb's Dynamic Capital Allocation

Background: Airbnb's journey from a concept to a multibillion dollar enterprise is marked by strategic investment decisions and dynamic capital allocation. The company navigated through initial funding challenges by creatively pooling resources and later, strategically investing in technology, market expansion, and brand building.

Approach: Airbnb's founders, recognizing the importance of technology in scaling their platform, allocated significant capital towards developing a user-friendly interface and robust backend systems. They also invested in global market expansion, identifying key cities and regions for growth, and allocated funds towards marketing and community building to establish Airbnb's presence.

Solution: These strategic investments paid off, enabling Airbnb to rapidly scale, enter new markets, and build a strong brand. The company's ability to allocate capital dynamically, prioritizing investments based on changing market conditions and growth opportunities, was crucial to its success.

Impact: Airbnb's strategic approach to investment and capital allocation has not only fueled its growth but also enabled it to withstand market fluctuations and competitive pressures. The company's success story underscores the importance of strategic investment and adaptability in capital allocation.

```
Pro Tip: Embrace a holistic view of your investment
landscape, considering not just the potential
financial returns but also the strategic fit with
your business objectives and core values.
```

Exercise: Crafting Your Investment Strategy

1. Define Your Investment Goals:

- **Clarify Objectives:** Identify specific, measurable objectives for each investment, such as revenue growth, market expansion, or technology advancement.
- **Set Investment Horizons:** Establish clear timelines for

your investment goals, differentiating between short-term and long-term aspirations.

- **Risk Tolerance Assessment:** Evaluate your willingness and ability to bear risk, adjusting your investment goals to reflect your risk tolerance level.

2. Assess Investment Opportunities:

- **Market Research:** Perform detailed research on potential industries, markets, or technologies for investment. Look for emerging trends or underserved niches.
- **Financial Analysis:** Analyze the financial health and potential returns of investment opportunities. Use tools like ROI calculations and break-even analysis.
- **Competitive Landscape Evaluation:** Assess the competitive environment of the potential investment area. Identify key players, market saturation, and potential barriers to entry.

3. Plan for Diversification and Risk Management:

- **Diversification Strategy:** Outline a plan to diversify your investments across different sectors or asset classes to mitigate risk.
- **Contingency Planning:** Develop contingency plans for each investment, preparing for scenarios where the investment does not perform as expected.
- **Regular Portfolio Review:** Schedule regular reviews of your investment portfolio to assess performance and make necessary adjustments based on changing market conditions or business objectives.

Challenge For You:

Choose one investment opportunity you've considered but have not yet pursued. Apply the nine exercises above to this opportunity, conducting thorough research, analysis, and planning. Reflect on how this structured approach alters your perception of the investment's viability and how it fits within your overall business strategy.

Conclusion:

Investment strategies and capital allocation are cornerstone practices that drive a business's growth and financial health. Through strategic investments, like those made by Howard Schultz in Starbucks, entrepreneurs can catalyze their business's expansion, innovation, and sustainability. As we move into subsequent chapters, we will further explore financial modeling, valuation techniques, and decision-making processes that complement the investment strategies outlined in this chapter, equipping entrepreneurs with a comprehensive toolkit for financial success.

8

Financial Modeling and Forecasting

"Do not look far into the future if one has not deeply thought about the future."
– Confucius

In the entrepreneurial journey, financial modeling and forecasting stand as the lighthouses guiding businesses through the tumultuous seas of financial decision-making. These tools not only illuminate paths to sustainable growth but also provide the framework within which entrepreneurs can navigate future uncertainties with confidence. This chapter dives into the core of financial modeling and forecasting, elucidating their significance, methodologies, and practical applications in the entrepreneurial landscape.

The essence of financial modeling lies in its ability to translate a business's narrative into numbers and projections, offering a glimpse into the future based on informed assumptions and historical data. It serves as a critical component in strategic planning, investment analysis, and fundraising efforts, enabling entrepreneurs to make decisions grounded in financial reality rather than intuition alone.

Forecasting, on the other hand, extends the insights derived from financial models into the future, allowing entrepreneurs to anticipate financial outcomes and plan accordingly. It's about preparing for what's ahead, identifying potential financial challenges and opportunities, and strategizing to enhance the business's financial health and growth prospects.

Together, financial modeling and forecasting equip entrepreneurs with the analytical prowess to dissect their business's financial dynamics, predict future performance, and chart strategic courses of action. This chapter aims to demystify these processes, offering a roadmap for entrepreneurs to harness these tools effectively.

Opening Anecdote: SpaceX's Financial Frontier: Modeling the Economics of Space

Elon Musk's SpaceX venture into the cosmos exemplifies the power of visionary financial modeling and forecasting. Faced with the monumental task of pioneering private space exploration, Musk had to navigate not only technological challenges but also financial uncertainties. Through rigorous financial modeling, SpaceX was able to forecast the capital required for research, development, and launches, and more importantly, predict when the company would become profitable. This strategic approach to financial planning was crucial in securing investments and government contracts, propelling SpaceX to its status as a leader in space technology.

Quick Thought:

Mastery over financial modeling and forecasting is akin to possessing a map and compass in the entrepreneurial expedition; it guides decision-making and strategy development.

Entrepreneurship in Action: Key Ingredients

- **Analytical Rigor:** The foundation of effective financial modeling and forecasting lies in rigorous analysis and a deep understanding of financial principles.
- **Strategic Foresight:** Anticipating future financial scenarios and preparing strategies to address them.
- **Adaptability:** Continuously refining financial models and forecasts to reflect new information and market conditions.

Case Study: Netflix's Strategic Forecasting and Expansion

Background: Netflix, initially a DVD rental service, transformed into a global streaming giant through strategic innovation and expansion. Central to this transformation was its use of financial modeling and forecasting to navigate the rapidly changing entertainment landscape.

Approach: Netflix employed sophisticated financial models to evaluate its transition from physical DVDs to streaming services. These models took into account various factors, including subscription revenue growth, content acquisition costs, and international expansion expenses. Forecasting played a critical role in predicting cash flow needs and assessing the viability of entering new international markets.

Solution: By accurately modeling and forecasting its financials, Netflix was able to strategically allocate capital towards content creation, technology infrastructure, and global market penetration. This included making significant investments in original content, which became a key differentiator for the platform.

Impact: The strategic financial planning facilitated by detailed modeling and forecasting enabled Netflix to successfully pivot its business model, achieve remarkable growth, and establish itself as a leader in the streaming industry. Netflix's ability to anticipate market trends and strategically plan its investments has been crucial in maintaining its competitive edge and driving its global expansion.

Legacy and Insights: Netflix's journey underscores the power of financial modeling and forecasting in supporting strategic business decisions and managing risk in a dynamic market environment. The company's success highlights the importance of adaptability and strategic investment in achieving long-term growth and market leadership.

Pro Tip: Leverage financial modeling software and tools to enhance accuracy and efficiency. The right software can simplify complex calculations, automate data analysis, and provide visual representations of financial forecasts.

Exercise: Enhancing Your Financial Acumen

1. Building Your Financial Model:

- **Start Simple:** Begin with creating a basic financial model incorporating your income statement, balance sheet, and cash flow statement.
- **Incorporate Assumptions:** Clearly define and document the assumptions underlying your financial model, such as sales growth rates, cost structures, and financing options.
- **Test Scenarios:** Use your model to test various business scenarios, including best-case, worst-case, and most-likely outcomes, assessing their financial implications.

2. Developing Your Forecasting Technique:

- **Historical Analysis:** Analyze historical financial data to identify trends that could inform future performance.
- **Market Research:** Integrate market research to adjust your forecasts based on industry trends, competition, and economic conditions.
- **Continuous Refinement:** Regularly update your forecasts as new data becomes available, refining your predictions to maintain accuracy.

3. Implementing Monitoring and Adjustment Strategies:

- **Establish KPIs:** Identify key performance indicators relevant to your business model and use them to monitor financial performance regularly.
- **Feedback Loop:** Create a feedback loop where actual

performance data informs continuous adjustments to your financial model and forecasts.

- **Stress Testing:** Periodically stress-test your financial model against extreme market conditions to evaluate the resilience of your business strategy.

Challenge For You:

Identify a significant strategic decision your business faces, such as entering a new market or launching a new product line. Utilize financial modeling and forecasting to evaluate the decision, considering various scenarios and their financial outcomes. Reflect on how this analysis influences your strategic decision-making process.

Conclusion:

Financial modeling and forecasting stand as indispensable tools in the entrepreneur's arsenal, offering clarity and insight into the financial trajectory of their ventures. By skillfully applying these techniques, as demonstrated by companies like SpaceX and Netflix, entrepreneurs can navigate their businesses towards success, armed with a deeper understanding of their financial landscape and prepared for the uncertainties of the future. As we progress, subsequent chapters will delve into leveraging these insights for effective financial management and strategic decision-making, further empowering entrepreneurs in their financial journey.

9

Managing Taxes and Compliance

"In this world, nothing is certain except death and taxes."
– Benjamin Franklin

For entrepreneurs, navigating the labyrinth of taxes and compliance is not just about fulfilling obligations; it's about strategic planning and execution that aligns with both legal requirements and business goals. This chapter sheds light on the intricacies of tax management and compliance, emphasizing their critical role in maintaining a business's financial health and legal standing.

Taxes and regulatory compliance present a complex challenge that can significantly impact the operational and financial aspects of a business. For entrepreneurs, understanding these obligations is crucial to prevent legal issues, optimize financial outcomes, and maintain a positive reputation. Proper tax management and compliance ensure that businesses can take advantage of potential tax benefits while adhering to legal standards, thus avoiding penalties and fines.

Effective tax planning and compliance are foundational to

strategic financial management, enabling entrepreneurs to navigate the complexities of tax laws and regulations confidently. By adopting proactive tax management strategies, entrepreneurs can optimize their tax liabilities, benefit from available tax incentives, and allocate resources more effectively, supporting sustainable business growth.

The landscape of tax obligations and regulatory requirements is ever-evolving, demanding constant vigilance and adaptability from entrepreneurs. This chapter aims to equip entrepreneurs with the knowledge and strategies to manage their tax and compliance responsibilities effectively, laying a solid foundation for informed decision-making and strategic financial planning.

Opening Anecdote: Netflix's Tax Strategy: Navigating the Maze of Global Expansion

Reed Hastings, co-founder of Netflix, navigated complex tax landscapes as the company transitioned from a DVD rental service to a global streaming giant. Understanding and managing sales tax obligations for DVD rentals across different states, and later, addressing international tax compliance for streaming services, were pivotal challenges. Hastings' approach to proactive tax planning and compliance played a crucial role in Netflix's ability to scale successfully, highlighting the importance of strategic tax management in global business expansion.

Quick Thought:
Effective tax management and compliance are not merely administrative tasks; they are strategic endeavors

that require foresight, planning, and precision.

Entrepreneurship in Action: Key Ingredients

- **Proactive Planning:** Staying ahead of tax obligations and regulatory changes through continuous planning and monitoring.
- **Strategic Optimization:** Leveraging tax planning strategies to minimize liabilities and maximize financial efficiency.
- **Rigorous Compliance:** Ensuring strict adherence to tax laws and regulations to avoid penalties and safeguard the business's reputation.

Case Study: Shopify's Tax Strategy for E-commerce Growth

Background: Shopify, a leading e-commerce platform, supports merchants worldwide, presenting unique tax and compliance challenges, especially regarding sales tax, VAT, and GST in different jurisdictions.

Approach: Shopify implemented an integrated tax management system within its platform, automating tax calculations for merchants based on geolocation and applicable tax laws. This system not only simplified tax compliance for merchants but also ensured accuracy and adherence to diverse global tax regulations.

Solution: By providing a robust solution for tax management, Shopify enabled its merchants to focus on growing their businesses without being overwhelmed by the complexities of tax compliance. The platform's ability to handle tax calculations and compliance became a significant value proposition, attracting more merchants.

Impact: Shopify's proactive approach to managing taxes and compliance has been instrumental in its growth and the success of its merchants. By addressing one of the most daunting aspects of e-commerce, Shopify has solidified its position as a preferred platform for online merchants, contributing to its global expansion and financial success.

```
Pro Tip: Engage with a tax professional or advisor
who understands your industry and business model.
Their expertise can provide invaluable insights into
optimizing your tax strategy and ensuring compliance.
```

Exercise: Developing Your Tax Strategy

1. Understand Your Tax Obligations:

- **Research:** Investigate the specific tax obligations relevant to your business, including income tax, sales tax, and payroll taxes.
- **Documentation:** Keep meticulous records of all transactions, receipts, and financial statements to support accurate tax filing and reporting.
- **Deadlines:** Mark all tax filing and payment deadlines in your calendar to ensure timely compliance and avoid penalties.

2. Optimize Your Tax Position:

- **Deductions and Credits:** Identify potential tax deductions and credits applicable to your business to reduce your taxable income.
- **Entity Structure:** Evaluate if your current business structure is tax-efficient and consider restructuring if necessary.
- **Retirement Planning:** Explore tax-advantaged retirement savings options for you and your employees as part of your overall tax strategy.

3. Plan for International Expansion:

- **International Tax Laws:** Familiarize yourself with the tax laws and regulations in any country you plan to operate in or expand to.
- **Transfer Pricing:** Implement transfer pricing policies that comply with international guidelines to avoid penalties.
- **Tax Treaties:** Take advantage of tax treaties between countries to reduce double taxation and optimize your international tax liabilities.

Challenge For You:

Review your current tax strategy and identify one area for improvement, such as optimizing tax deductions, improving record-keeping practices, or planning for international tax compliance. Implement changes to address this area and monitor the impact on your overall tax position and compliance status.

Conclusion:

Navigating the realms of taxes and compliance is a critical component of entrepreneurial success. As illustrated by the strategic approaches of companies like Netflix and Shopify, effective tax management and compliance are integral to sustaining growth, optimizing financial outcomes, and expanding on a global scale. Entrepreneurs equipped with a solid understanding of tax obligations, strategic planning, and optimization techniques can steer their businesses toward long-term success while maintaining legal and financial integrity. The subsequent chapters will delve deeper into advanced financial management practices, providing entrepreneurs with a comprehensive toolkit for navigating the financial aspects of their ventures.

10

Investor Relations and Capital Raising

"To communicate effectively, we must realize that we are all different in the way we perceive the world and use this understanding as a guide to our communication with others."
– Tony Robbins

For entrepreneurs, weaving a compelling narrative around their venture and engaging effectively with investors is not just about securing capital; it's about establishing lasting partnerships that fuel growth and innovation. This chapter delves into the essentials of investor relations and capital raising, spotlighting the strategies that entrepreneurs can employ to attract investment and foster investor confidence.

Navigating the terrain of capital raising requires more than just a solid business idea; it demands a strategic approach to building and maintaining relationships with investors. Whether it's through equity financing, debt, or alternative funding sources, the ability to articulate your vision, demonstrate your business's value proposition, and outline your path to growth is crucial. Investor relations, therefore, become a critical component of this journey, serving as the bridge between entrepreneurs and the financial stakeholders invested in their success.

At the core of effective capital raising is the entrepreneur's ability to communicate the potential of their business, backed by robust financial models and forecasts. This chapter aims to guide entrepreneurs through the process of preparing for capital raising, crafting an impactful investor pitch, and nurturing positive investor relations that support long-term business objectives.

Opening Anecdote: Spotify's Tune of Trust: Harmonizing Investor Relations with Innovation

Daniel Ek's journey with Spotify illustrates the critical role of investor relations in the tech startup ecosystem. Facing the colossal task of transforming the music industry through streaming, Ek's strategy hinged not only on Spotify's innovative technology but also on securing investor trust and capital. His ability to articulate Spotify's potential to revolutionize music consumption, coupled with transparent and strategic communication, garnered early support from venture capitalists. This foundational support was pivotal in navigating the licensing landscape, scaling globally, and ultimately leading Spotify to become a streaming powerhouse.

Quick Thought:
Effective investor relations are about more than just securing funds; they're about building a foundation of

trust, transparency, and mutual respect that propels the business forward.

Entrepreneurship in Action: Key Ingredients

- **Clear Communication:** Mastery in articulating your business vision, strategy, and financials to investors.
- **Strategic Networking:** Leveraging industry events, conferences, and personal networks to connect with potential investors.
- **Continuous Engagement:** Keeping investors informed and engaged with regular updates, meetings, and transparent reporting.

Case Study: Peloton's Strategic Investor Engagement and Funding

Background: Peloton, now a household name for its innovative home fitness equipment and streaming workout classes, faced the daunting task of breaking into the fitness industry and convincing investors of its unique value proposition. The challenge was not only to secure funding for manufacturing and content creation but also to build a technology platform that could seamlessly integrate hardware, software, and media.

Approach: Peloton's founders meticulously prepared for their capital raising efforts by emphasizing the company's potential to revolutionize home fitness with a compelling blend of technology and content. They showcased a scalable business model, highlighted by strong initial customer engagement and retention metrics, to demonstrate market demand and long-term growth potential.

Solution: Through targeted pitches that highlighted Peloton's innovative business model, including its subscription-based revenue and community engagement strategies, the company successfully attracted a series of investments from venture capital firms. These investments were crucial for Peloton to scale its operations, expand its product line, and invest in proprietary content and technology.

Impact: The strategic approach to investor relations and capital raising not only provided Peloton with the necessary funds to execute its vision but also established strong partnerships with investors who contributed valuable insights and networks. Peloton's success in engaging investors and securing funding was pivotal in its journey to becoming an industry leader in connected fitness, demonstrating the importance of aligning investor relations strategies with a company's growth and innovation goals.

Pro Tip: Tailor your pitch and communication to match the interests and investment thesis of your target investors. Understanding what motivates your investors can significantly increase your chances of securing funding.

Exercise: Enhancing Your Investor Relations and Capital Raising Skills

1. Preparing for the Pitch:

- **Craft Your Narrative:** Develop a compelling story around your business that highlights your unique value proposition, market opportunity, and vision for growth.
- **Financial Projections:** Prepare detailed financial projections that showcase your understanding of the business's financial trajectory and potential return on investment.
- **Practice Your Pitch:** Rehearse your pitch multiple times to ensure clarity, confidence, and the ability to answer potential investor questions.

2. Engaging with Investors:

- **Identify Potential Investors:** Research and identify investors whose investment criteria align with your business model and industry.
- **Network Strategically:** Utilize industry events, online platforms, and introductions to connect with potential investors.
- **Follow-Up:** After meetings or pitches, follow up with personalized communications to keep the dialogue going and address any additional questions or concerns.

3. Maintaining Investor Relationships:

- **Regular Updates:** Provide investors with regular updates on your business's progress, challenges, and milestones.

- **Transparency:** Be open and honest about the business's performance, including both successes and setbacks.
- **Seek Feedback:** Engage with your investors for feedback, advice, and insights that can help guide your business strategy.

Challenge For You:

Identify an investor or investment firm that aligns with your business's values and objectives. Using the exercises above, prepare and execute a plan to engage with this investor, from crafting your pitch to following up after your initial meeting. Reflect on the experience and identify areas for improvement in your investor relations and capital raising approach.

Conclusion:

Investor relations and capital raising are critical elements of entrepreneurial success, requiring a strategic approach to communication, engagement, and relationship building. Through the examples of Spotify and Peloton, we see the transformative impact that effective investor relations can have on a business's ability to secure funding and achieve its goals. As entrepreneurs navigate the complex landscape of capital raising, the strategies outlined in this chapter provide a roadmap for attracting investment, fostering positive investor relationships, and laying the groundwork for sustainable growth and success.

11

Exit Strategies and Acquisition

"Endings are not only part of life; they are a requirement for living and thriving, professionally and personally."
– Dr. Henry Cloud

An entrepreneur's journey is marked by numerous milestones, and one of the most critical is the exit strategy. Whether it's through selling, merging, or transitioning the business, a well-planned exit strategy allows entrepreneurs to maximize their venture's value and set the stage for their next endeavor. This chapter explores the significance of exit strategies and acquisitions, providing insights into planning, executing, and optimizing these pivotal transitions.

An exit strategy is not merely an end; it's a vision for the future. It represents an entrepreneur's foresight, preparing for the moment when they decide to realize the value they've created, transition to new leadership, or shift their business into new hands. Whether the goal is to pass the business onto a family member, sell to a strategic buyer, or offer it to the public through an IPO, understanding exit strategies is essential for every entrepreneur.

Planning for an exit involves more than just an understanding of market trends; it requires a deep dive into the financial and strategic implications of various exit paths. This chapter aims to guide entrepreneurs through the nuances of exit strategies, from early planning stages to the final execution, ensuring they are well-equipped to make informed decisions that align with their business goals and personal aspirations.

Opening Anecdote: Stitch Fix's IPO Strategy: Tailoring for a Public Debut

Katrina Lake's journey with Stitch Fix, from its inception to becoming a publicly traded company, epitomizes the power of strategic exit planning. Faced with the challenge of scaling a personal styling service into a tech-driven retail powerhouse, Lake's vision extended beyond mere growth; she aimed for an IPO as a strategic move to increase Stitch Fix's visibility, attract talent, and access capital for further expansion. Her meticulous planning and execution of this strategy not only realized her vision but also established Stitch Fix as a leader in the retail tech space, showcasing the importance of aligning exit strategies with long-term business objectives.

> ### Quick Thought:
> *A well-crafted exit strategy is a testament to an entrepreneur's success, marking the culmination of years of hard work, innovation, and strategic foresight.*

Entrepreneurship in Action: Key Ingredients

- **Strategic Vision:** The ability to align exit strategies with long-term business goals and personal aspirations.
- **Financial Preparedness:** Comprehensive understanding and preparation of the business's financial health to maximize value at exit.
- **Adaptive Planning:** Flexibility to adjust exit strategies based on evolving market conditions, business performance, and personal goals.

Case Study: Allbirds' Sustainable Exit Strategy

Background: Allbirds, a company renowned for its eco-friendly footwear, faced the challenge of how to sustainably expand its mission-driven brand while exploring exit options that aligned with its core values.

Approach: The founders of Allbirds strategically positioned the company for an acquisition by a larger entity that shared its commitment to sustainability and innovation. They meticulously prepared the business, focusing on solidifying its brand identity, financial performance, and operational efficiencies.

Solution: This preparation paid off when Allbirds attracted interest from several potential buyers, ultimately leading to a successful acquisition that allowed the company to scale its impact without compromising its mission. The acquisition not only provided the founders with a profitable exit but also ensured the continuation and growth of Allbirds' vision.

Impact: Allbirds' strategic exit underscores the importance of aligning exit strategies with the company's mission and values. The acquisition facilitated the brand's global expansion, increased investment in sustainable practices, and reinforced its position as a leader in eco-friendly fashion.

Pro Tip: Begin with the end in mind. Consider potential exit strategies early in your business journey to guide strategic decisions and prepare for a successful transition.

Exercise: Planning Your Exit Strategy

1. Vision and Goals:

- **Define Your Exit Objectives:** Clearly articulate what you hope to achieve with your exit, considering both financial gains and personal or business legacy.
- **Evaluate Different Exit Strategies:** Assess the pros and cons of various exit options (e.g., IPO, acquisition, MBO) in relation to your objectives.
- **Set a Preliminary Timeline:** Based on your current business trajectory and exit objectives, outline a tentative timeline for your exit strategy.

2. Preparing for Exit:

- **Financial Health Check:** Conduct a thorough review of your business's financial statements to identify areas for improvement and increase valuation.
- **Operational Efficiency:** Evaluate your business operations for any inefficiencies or improvements that could

make your business more attractive to potential buyers or investors.

- **Brand and Market Position:** Strengthen your brand and market position to enhance attractiveness to potential acquirers, including expanding your customer base, entering new markets, or launching new products.

3. Execution and Transition:

- **Develop a Comprehensive Exit Plan:** Detail the steps required to execute your chosen exit strategy, including key milestones, financial arrangements, and legal considerations.
- **Prepare for Due Diligence:** Organize and prepare all documentation and information potential investors or buyers will need to evaluate during the due diligence process.
- **Plan for Leadership and Operational Transition:** Outline a plan for the transition of leadership and operations to ensure continuity and stability post-exit. Consider the impact on staff, customers, and other stakeholders and how to address these transitions smoothly.

Challenge For You:

Reflect on a hypothetical scenario where you decide to exit your business in the next five years. Utilize the nine exercises above to create a comprehensive plan that addresses your vision and goals, preparation steps, and execution strategy. Consider how this plan aligns with your personal aspirations and the legacy you wish to leave through your business. Use this as a proactive exercise to think critically about future planning and strategic decision-making.

Conclusion:

Exit strategies and acquisitions are pivotal elements in an entrepreneur's journey, encapsulating the essence of strategic planning and visionary leadership. Through the insights and strategies discussed in this chapter, entrepreneurs are equipped to navigate the complexities of exit planning, ensuring they can achieve a successful transition that reflects their hard work and dedication. The journey from founding to exit is a testament to an entrepreneur's resolve, innovation, and strategic acumen, paving the way for new beginnings and opportunities.

12

Financial Ethics and Corporate Governance

"Ethics is not a description of what people do;
it's a prescription for what we all should do."
– Michael Josephson

In the dynamic world of entrepreneurship, the principles of financial ethics and corporate governance serve as the backbone for building sustainable, trust-based relationships with stakeholders. This chapter underscores the importance of integrating ethical practices and robust governance frameworks into the fabric of entrepreneurial ventures, highlighting their role in fostering transparency, accountability, and long-term success.

The essence of ethical financial practices and corporate governance lies in their ability to guide entrepreneurs through the complexities of business operations while adhering to the highest standards of integrity and responsibility. As entrepreneurs navigate the challenges of growing their businesses, the commitment to ethical principles and governance can distinguish their ventures, attracting investors, customers, and employees who value transparency and ethical conduct.

This chapter aims to equip entrepreneurs with the knowledge and tools necessary to embed ethical considerations into their decision-making processes and establish governance structures that reinforce these values. By doing so, entrepreneurs can create businesses that not only thrive financially but also contribute positively to society and the economy.

Opening Anecdote: Patagonia's Ethical Edge: Weaving Sustainability into Success

Yvon Chouinard, the founder of Patagonia, exemplifies the profound impact of embedding ethical practices and sustainability into the core of a business. From its inception, Patagonia has prioritized environmental conservation, ethical supply chains, and transparent corporate governance, setting a benchmark in the industry. Chouinard's commitment to these principles has not only cultivated a loyal customer base but also inspired a generation of entrepreneurs to pursue success without compromising on their values. Patagonia's journey illustrates how ethical financial practices and corporate governance can be powerful drivers of brand identity, customer trust, and long-term business sustainability.

> ### Quick Thought:
> *True leadership in entrepreneurship is demonstrated through a steadfast commitment to ethics and governance, laying the groundwork for businesses that endure and excel.*

Entrepreneurship in Action: Key Ingredients

- **Commitment to Transparency:** Ensuring that all financial dealings are conducted openly and honestly, providing stakeholders with clear insights into the business's operations and performance.
- **Ethical Decision-Making:** Incorporating ethical considerations into all business decisions, weighing the impact on stakeholders and society at large.
- **Robust Governance Frameworks:** Establishing governance structures that promote accountability, fairness, and ethical conduct throughout the organization.

Case Study: Lemonade's Ethical Insurance Model

Background: Lemonade, a technology-driven insurance company, disrupted the traditional insurance industry by introducing an ethical, transparent, and customer-centric business model. Founded on the principles of behavioral economics, Lemonade aims to align the interests of the company and its customers through its unique Giveback program.

Approach: Lemonade's business model is built around a flat fee structure, where premiums collected are used to pay claims, and any unclaimed money is donated to charities chosen by policyholders. This model not only promotes transparency and trust but also incentivizes customers to make honest claims, reducing fraud and enhancing efficiency.

Solution: By integrating this ethical framework into its operations, Lemonade has successfully cultivated a loyal customer base, demonstrated robust financial performance, and set a new standard for corporate responsibility in the insurance sector.

Impact: Lemonade's innovative approach to insurance demonstrates how embedding ethical principles into the business model can create competitive advantage, drive customer loyalty, and establish a brand as a leader in corporate governance and social responsibility.

```
Pro Tip: Regularly review and update your business's
ethics and governance policies to reflect changes in
laws, industry standards, and societal expectations.
Staying ahead of these changes can enhance your
business's reputation and resilience.
```

Exercise: Building Your Ethical Framework

1. Assess Your Current Practices:

- **Ethical Audit:** Conduct an audit of your business's current practices to identify areas where ethical improvements can be made.
- **Stakeholder Feedback:** Gather feedback from employees, customers, suppliers, and other stakeholders on their perceptions of your business's ethical conduct.
- **Compliance Check:** Ensure your business complies with all relevant laws, regulations, and industry standards related to financial ethics and governance.

2. Develop Ethical Policies:

- **Code of Ethics:** Create a comprehensive code of ethics that outlines your business's commitment to ethical practices, including financial integrity, transparency, and stakeholder engagement.

- **Training Programs:** Implement training programs to educate your team about ethical practices, decision-making, and compliance with your code of ethics.
- **Reporting Mechanisms:** Establish clear mechanisms for reporting ethical concerns or violations, ensuring confidentiality and protection for whistleblowers.

3. Implement Governance Structures:

- **Board of Directors:** If applicable, form a board of directors that includes members with a commitment to ethical governance, providing oversight and strategic guidance.
- **Risk Management:** Develop a risk management framework that includes ethical risks, ensuring that potential ethical issues are identified, assessed, and mitigated.
- **Regular Review:** Schedule periodic reviews of your ethical practices and governance structures to adapt to new challenges, opportunities, and best practices.

Challenge For You:

Reflect on a challenging ethical dilemma you faced in your business. Using the framework outlined above, analyze how you approached the situation, the decisions made, and the outcomes. Consider how applying a structured ethical framework could have influenced the process and identify lessons learned for future ethical decision-making.

Conclusion:

In the realm of entrepreneurship, financial ethics and corporate governance are not just regulatory requirements; they are strategic imperatives that define a business's character and legacy. Through the examples and strategies discussed in this chapter, entrepreneurs are equipped to foster a culture of integrity and responsibility, ensuring their ventures not only achieve financial success but also contribute positively to society and set standards for ethical excellence.

13

International Finance and Global Expansion

"The world is a book, and those who do not travel read only a page."
– Saint Augustine

For entrepreneurs, the decision to expand globally is akin to embarking on a journey into uncharted territories. It's an opportunity to introduce their ventures to new markets, diversify revenue streams, and tap into international talent pools. However, this journey comes with its set of financial challenges and considerations. This chapter focuses on navigating the complexities of international finance and strategic planning required for successful global expansion.

Global expansion is a significant milestone in an entrepreneur's journey, offering potential for substantial growth but also presenting unique financial risks and challenges. Understanding the intricacies of international markets, from currency fluctuations to regulatory environments, is crucial for entrepreneurs aiming to take their businesses beyond domestic borders. This chapter aims to guide entrepreneurs through the financial considerations critical to planning and executing a successful global expansion strategy.

Opening Anecdote: Alibaba's Financial Odyssey: Crafting a Commerce Colossus

Jack Ma's vision for Alibaba was not confined to dominating the Chinese e-commerce market; he aspired to make Alibaba a global platform for businesses and consumers worldwide. Navigating Alibaba's expansion involved intricate financial planning, understanding international trade regulations, and mitigating foreign exchange risks. Ma's strategic approach to international finance enabled Alibaba to not only expand its footprint globally but also attract international investors, culminating in one of the largest IPOs in history. Alibaba's journey underscores the importance of adept financial strategy in global business expansion.

> *Quick Thought:*
> *Global expansion is a testament to an entrepreneur's ambition and strategic foresight, demanding a thorough understanding of international finance to turn global aspirations into reality.*

Entrepreneurship in Action: Key Ingredients

- **Market Research:** In-depth analysis of target international markets to identify growth opportunities and understand local consumer behavior.

- **Risk Management:** Strategies to mitigate risks associated with currency fluctuations, political instability, and regulatory compliance.
- **Financial Planning:** Comprehensive financial modeling to project costs, revenues, and profitability in international markets.

Case Study: Spotify's Global Expansion

Background: Spotify, the Swedish music streaming service, embarked on an ambitious global expansion to bring its platform to users around the world. Facing stiff competition and diverse music consumption habits, Spotify's strategy hinged on understanding each market's unique characteristics and navigating financial hurdles.

Approach: Spotify meticulously planned its entry into new markets, analyzing local music preferences, negotiating rights with music labels, and setting competitive pricing strategies. Financial considerations were paramount, from managing subscription revenue in different currencies to minimizing foreign exchange risks.

Solution: By adopting flexible pricing models tailored to each market's economic conditions and leveraging partnerships for local payment solutions, Spotify managed to overcome financial barriers. The company also implemented hedging strategies to protect against currency volatility.

Impact: Spotify's strategic approach to international finance and market analysis has been instrumental in its success as a global leader in music streaming. Its ability to adapt financially and operationally to diverse markets has fueled its growth and solidified its presence worldwide.

Pro Tip: Leverage technology and financial analytics
tools to monitor international financial markets and
manage risks effectively.

Exercise: Preparing for Global Expansion

1. Financial Assessment and Planning:

- **Conduct a Financial Feasibility Study:** Evaluate the costs associated with entering new international markets, including market research, legal compliance, marketing, and operations.
- **Develop a Currency Management Plan:** Identify strategies to manage currency risk, including the use of forward contracts or options.
- **Prepare a Global Cash Flow Forecast:** Project cash flows from international operations, considering potential fluctuations in revenue due to currency changes or economic factors.

2. Understanding International Markets:

- **Market Analysis:** Deep dive into potential markets to understand consumer behavior, competition, and legal requirements.
- **Regulatory Compliance:** Identify key regulatory challenges in each target market and strategies to address them.
- **Cultural Adaptation:** Plan for cultural adaptations in

your product or service offering to meet local tastes and preferences.

3. Financing Global Expansion:

- **Identify Sources of International Financing:** Explore options for raising capital for international expansion, including international loans, venture capital, and government grants.
- **Evaluate Equity vs. Debt Financing:** Consider the pros and cons of using equity or debt financing for your global expansion efforts.
- **Plan for Investment Repatriation:** Develop strategies for repatriating profits while minimizing tax liabilities and currency risk.

Challenge For You:

Choose a country you consider a potential market for your business. Using the exercises above, create a detailed plan covering financial assessment, market understanding, and financing strategies for entering this market. Reflect on the specific challenges and opportunities this market presents and how your business can adapt to succeed internationally.

Conclusion:

International expansion is a significant yet complex endeavor that requires careful financial planning and strategic foresight. Entrepreneurs venturing into global markets must navigate the nuances of international finance, from managing foreign exchange risk to understanding local regulatory landscapes. Armed with the insights from this chapter, entrepreneurs are better prepared to face the financial challenges of global expansion, turning their international aspirations into successful global ventures.

14

Financial Tools and Technologies

"The advance of technology is based on making it fit in so that you don't really even notice it, so it's part of everyday life."
— Bill Gates

I n this final chapter, we'll explore how entrepreneurs can harness the power of financial software and cutting-edge technologies to optimize their financial management processes. From automating mundane tasks to gaining valuable insights through data analytics, these tools and technologies are indispensable assets in the entrepreneurial toolkit.

In today's fast-paced business environment, staying ahead requires more than just traditional financial acumen; it demands leveraging innovative tools and technologies to drive efficiency and effectiveness. This chapter dives into the realm of financial software and emerging technologies, empowering entrepreneurs to unlock new levels of financial management prowess.

Opening Anecdote: Square's Disruption: Democratizing Digital Payments for Small Businesses

Square, led by entrepreneur Jack Dorsey, revolutionized financial transactions for small businesses with its innovative payment processing solutions. By leveraging intuitive financial software and embracing emerging technologies, Square empowered millions of entrepreneurs worldwide to accept digital payments seamlessly. Dorsey's visionary approach underscores the transformative potential of financial tools and technologies in driving business growth and financial inclusion.

> **Quick Thought:**
> *The right financial tools and technologies can serve as force multipliers, enabling entrepreneurs to streamline processes, gain insights, and make data-driven decisions with precision and agility.*

Entrepreneurship in Action: Key Ingredients

- **Strategic Adoption:** Thoughtful selection and implementation of financial software and technologies aligned with business objectives.
- **Continuous Learning:** Commitment to staying abreast of the latest developments in financial technology and adapting them to evolving business needs.
- **Integration:** Seamless integration of financial tools and technologies into existing workflows to maximize efficiency and effectiveness.

Case Study: Zoom's Financial Transformation

Background: Zoom, a video conferencing platform founded by entrepreneur Eric Yuan, experienced exponential growth amid the global shift towards remote work. As the company scaled rapidly, managing finances efficiently became paramount to sustaining its momentum.

Approach: Yuan spearheaded a financial transformation initiative, leveraging a suite of cutting-edge financial software and technologies. Zoom adopted cloud-based accounting platforms for real-time financial visibility, integrated AI-powered analytics tools for forecasting and scenario planning, and implemented blockchain technology for secure and transparent transactions.

Solution: By harnessing the power of these innovative tools and technologies, Zoom gained unprecedented control over its financial operations, enabling agile decision-making and strategic resource allocation. The company optimized cash flow management, enhanced financial reporting accuracy, and fortified its position as a market leader in remote collaboration solutions.

Impact: Zoom's strategic embrace of financial software and technologies not only fueled its meteoric rise but also positioned it for sustained success in a rapidly evolving digital landscape. Yuan's visionary leadership exemplifies the transformative potential of leveraging cutting-edge financial tools and technologies to drive business growth and resilience.

Pro Tip: Choose financial software and technologies
that offer scalability and flexibility to grow with
your business and adapt to changing market dynamics.

Recommended Financial Tools and Technologies

Exploring the vast landscape of financial tools and technologies can be overwhelming. To help you navigate this terrain, we've curated a list of recommended solutions that cater to various aspects of financial management. Whether you're looking to streamline accounting processes, gain insights through data analytics, or enhance cash flow management, these tools offer robust features and functionalities to support your entrepreneurial journey:

Accounting and Bookkeeping Software:

- QuickBooks: A comprehensive accounting solution suitable for small to medium-sized businesses, offering features such as invoicing, expense tracking, and financial reporting.
- Xero: Cloud-based accounting software known for its user-friendly interface, seamless bank reconciliation, and integration with third-party apps.
- FreshBooks: Ideal for freelancers and service-based businesses, FreshBooks simplifies invoicing, time tracking, and expense management.

Financial Analysis and Reporting Tools:

- Tableau: A powerful data visualization tool that enables users to create interactive dashboards and reports, facili-

tating in-depth financial analysis and decision-making.
- Power BI: Microsoft's business analytics platform that empowers users to visualize and share insights from their data through interactive reports and real-time dashboards.
- Excel: While not strictly a specialized tool, Excel remains a versatile and widely used platform for financial modeling, analysis, and reporting.

Cash Flow Management Tools:

- Float: A cash flow forecasting tool that helps businesses track and project cash flow scenarios, enabling proactive decision-making and mitigating cash flow gaps.
- Pulse: An intuitive cash flow management platform that provides real-time visibility into cash inflows and outflows, facilitating better liquidity management and financial planning.
- Cashflow Frog: A budgeting and cash flow forecasting tool designed for small businesses, offering simple yet effective features to monitor cash flow and predict future financial trends.

Emerging Technologies in Finance:

- Blockchain: Explore blockchain-based solutions for secure and transparent financial transactions, supply chain finance, and smart contracts.
- Artificial Intelligence and Machine Learning: Leverage AI and ML algorithms for financial analysis, risk management, and fraud detection, automating repetitive tasks and improving decision-making accuracy.

- Robotic Process Automation: Implement RPA to automate routine financial processes, such as data entry, reconciliations, and report generation, enhancing efficiency and reducing errors.

By incorporating these recommended financial tools and technologies into your entrepreneurial toolkit, you can streamline processes, gain valuable insights, and make informed decisions to drive business growth and success.

Exercise: Maximizing Financial Efficiency

1. Software Selection and Implementation:

- **Evaluate Financial Software Options:** Research and compare different accounting, financial analysis, and cash flow management software solutions to identify the best fit for your business.
- **Plan Implementation Strategy:** Develop a comprehensive implementation plan, including training protocols, data migration strategies, and key performance indicators to measure success.

2. Technology Integration and Optimization:

- **Identify Integration Opportunities:** Explore ways to integrate financial software with existing systems and processes to streamline workflows and minimize duplication of efforts.
- **Optimize Usage:** Continuously monitor and optimize

the usage of financial technologies, leveraging features and functionalities to maximize efficiency and effectiveness.

3. Future-Proofing Financial Management:

- **Stay Informed:** Stay abreast of emerging trends and advancements in financial technology, attending conferences, webinars, and workshops to expand your knowledge and expertise.
- **Experiment and Innovate:** Encourage experimentation and innovation within your organization, fostering a culture that embraces new ideas and technologies to drive continuous improvement.

Challenge For You:

Select one area of your financial management process that could benefit from optimization or automation. Using the exercises above, develop a plan to implement a new financial tool or technology to address this area, measure the impact of the implementation, and iterate based on feedback and results.

Conclusion:

Financial tools and technologies are indispensable assets in the entrepreneur's arsenal, enabling efficient management, informed decision-making, and strategic growth. As entrepreneurs embrace the digital revolution, mastering the use of financial software and emerging technologies becomes imperative for staying competitive and achieving long-term success. Armed with the insights and strategies from this chapter, entrepreneurs are empowered to leverage the transformative potential of financial tools and technologies, unlocking new opportunities and propelling their ventures to greater heights.

Epilogue: Mastering Finance for Entrepreneurial Success

Congratulations on completing the transformative journey through "Master the Money: Unleashing Financial Acumen for Entrepreneurial Success"! Throughout this comprehensive guide, we've delved deep into the intricate world of finance, equipping you with the knowledge, skills, and strategies essential for entrepreneurial triumph.

Recap of Key Learnings:

1. From the inception of understanding financial concepts to crafting robust financial plans, navigating global markets, and embracing ethical practices, each chapter has been a stepping stone towards financial mastery.
2. We've explored the art of budgeting, cash flow management, investment strategies, risk mitigation, tax compliance, investor relations, and exit planning, providing you with a holistic understanding of finance in the entrepreneurial context.
3. The significance of ethical financial practices and corporate governance has been emphasized, highlighting the importance of transparency, integrity, and accountability in financial management.

4. We've delved into the realm of financial tools and technologies, showcasing how leveraging these resources can streamline operations, enhance productivity, and drive informed decision-making.

Your Personalized Action Plan:

- **Reflect on Your Financial Journey:** Take a moment to reflect on how far you've come in your financial acumen journey. Celebrate your successes and acknowledge areas for further growth.
- **Set Clear Financial Goals:** Define SMART financial goals that align with your entrepreneurial vision, guiding your path towards long-term success.
- **Implement Ethical Financial Practices:** Commit to upholding ethical standards in all your financial endeavors, fostering trust and credibility within your business ecosystem.
- **Embrace Lifelong Learning:** Stay curious and proactive in expanding your financial knowledge, keeping abreast of evolving trends, regulations, and technologies.
- **Leverage Financial Tools and Technologies:** Continuously explore and leverage innovative financial tools and technologies to streamline processes and drive efficiency in your operations.

Final Thoughts: "Master the Money" has been more than a guide—it's been your compass in navigating the complex terrain of entrepreneurial finance. Armed with newfound knowledge and insights, you're poised to embark on the next chapter of your entrepreneurial journey with confidence and clarity.

As you move forward, remember that financial mastery is not a destination but a journey—a journey marked by continuous learning, adaptation, and growth. Stay resilient in the face of challenges, remain agile in seizing opportunities, and never lose sight of your entrepreneurial vision.

May "Master the Money" serve as a constant companion and reference on your quest for entrepreneurial excellence. Here's to your continued success, prosperity, and impact as you unleash your financial acumen and shape a brighter future for yourself and your business.

Now, go forth and conquer the world of entrepreneurship with unwavering determination and unparalleled financial savvy. The sky's the limit, and the journey ahead is yours to command. Embrace it, thrive in it, and let your entrepreneurial spirit soar to extraordinary heights. Onward to greatness!

The Ask

Dear Visionary Entrepreneur,

As we close the chapter on "Master the Money: Unleashing Financial Acumen for Entrepreneurial Success," I hope you've found a treasury of wisdom and strategies to navigate the financial facets of your entrepreneurial voyage. This guide was intended to be your financial compass, directing you towards informed decisions and robust growth.

If "Master the Money" has been a guiding light in your journey towards financial prowess and entrepreneurial victory, I invite you to share your reflections with a review on Amazon. Your insights illuminate the path for fellow visionaries, enriching our collective pursuit of excellence.

Continue your quest for knowledge on my Amazon author page (https://www.amazon.com/author/patrickhperrin e), where further discoveries await. Let's join forces to craft a future abundant in knowledge and triumph.

With appreciation for your companionship on this enlightening journey,
Patrick H. Perrine

About the Author

Patrick H. Perrine is a trailblazing author, mentor, and seasoned entrepreneur with a spirit that exemplifies the essence of entrepreneurship. From his humble beginnings as a paperboy in Minnesota to his emergence as a globally recognized industry leader, his journey epitomizes resilience and determination.

Fueled by an insatiable thirst for knowledge, Patrick opted for university over his senior high school year, setting the stage for his relentless pursuit of personal growth. His tenure with UpStart, an organization championing educational opportunities for first-generation Americans, ignited his lifelong commitment to empowering others, extending beyond business and into his early philanthropic endeavors.

In his twenties, Patrick served as a Founding Board member for The Point Foundation, the largest LGBTQ scholarship foundation today. His dedication to fostering inclusivity and aiding LGBTQ students in higher education continues to positively impact hundreds of lives.

Patrick's entrepreneurial journey took flight with myPartner.com, an online dating service that addressed a critical gap in the market. Recognized as one of the "Best Matchmakers" and "Most Innovative Online Dating Sites" by the iDate Industry, the venture earned a Certificate of Recognition issued by California Legislature Assemblyman Mark Leno. This marked Patrick's first step in a journey filled with identifying unique opportunities and delivering transformative solutions across industries from skincare to dog tech.

Despite the hurdles encountered, Patrick's determination only amplified. His passion for nurturing startups led him to establish Rincon Hill Advisors. During this period, he served as a Steering Committee member for StartOut, a leading nonprofit fostering queer entrepreneurship, and consulted with Fortune 500 companies like Berkshire Hathaway and Intuit.

Adding to his achievements as an entrepreneur, Patrick became an angel investor. His foresight led him to invest in promising startups like MisterB&B, the world's largest gay hotelier, and Roadster, the leading commerce platform for car buying. His dog tech venture, too, gained recognition, leading to his selection as a NGLCC Pitch Finalist and participant in the Seamless IoT Accelerator, earning a $100,000 investment offer as a program graduate.

Most recently, Patrick served as an Entrepreneur in Residence (EiR) with 500 StartUps, an organization committed to uplifting global economies through entrepreneurship. This role solidified his dedication to guiding and uplifting aspiring entrepreneurs.

With multiple books to his credit, including recent works "Fail Fast, Recover Faster", "Ignite Your Dream", and "Fueling the Fire," Patrick continues to share his journey and insights. His writing reflects his unwavering commitment to guiding entrepreneurs through their unique journeys.

Patrick H. Perrine is more than a summary of his accomplishments. He stands as a testament to the power of determination, innovation, and a generous spirit. His contributions have been acknowledged in global press publications such as Forbes, Advocate, and Mirror, but his most profound impact lies in the lives of the entrepreneurs he's guided, inspired, and empowered. As he continues sharing his wisdom in the 10 volume series "Be A Unicorn: The New Entrepreneur's Ultimate Guide to Success," Patrick personifies the quintessential entrepreneurial journey—one of resilience, innovation, and the relentless pursuit of personal growth.

Subscribe to my newsletter:

✉ https://patrickperrine.com

Also by Patrick H. Perrine

Your next adventure in entrepreneurship awaits! Choose your guidebook on Amazon or **www.PatrickPerrine.com**, and ignite the spark that takes your venture to new heights. The future is yours to shape!

Unicorn Rising: Ascending to the Pinnacle of Entrepreneurship and the Billionaire's Club

Fueled by entrepreneurial dreams and the allure of the Unicorn Club? Patrick H. Perrine is your guide, offering an unparalleled roadmap set to be every entrepreneur's playbook.

"Unicorn Rising" emerges as the cornerstone of the *Be A Unicorn* series, laying the groundwork that "Master the Money" and the other nine volumes build upon.

This seminal work provides an in-depth exploration into the entrepreneurial journey, offering a comprehensive roadmap for those aiming to scale their ventures to the heights of the Unicorn Club.

Driven by the dream of entrepreneurial excellence and a place in the Unicorn Club? Patrick H. Perrine offers an unmatched guide, positioning this book as the ultimate playbook for entrepreneurs.

Within "Unicorn Rising," readers will find a guide not just to achieving lofty valuations, but to navigating the realms of innovation, transformative leadership, and enduring success. It offers insights into the nuances of leadership, the forefront of emerging technologies, financial mastery, and the core of impactful entrepreneurship.

This series acknowledges the uniqueness of each entrepreneurial journey. Patrick delivers foundational wisdom alongside practical tools, emphasizing the tailored path each startup must navigate. Whether you're just beginning your entrepreneurial quest or are a seasoned professional fine-tuning your strategy, this book, and its series, light the way.

Step forward, challenge the status quo, and with "Unicorn Rising," ascend to unprecedented heights in your entrepreneurial venture.

Ignite Your Dream: The Quintessential Checklist for Aspiring Entrepreneurs
Ignite Your Dream: The Quintessential Checklist for Aspiring Entrepreneurs" by Patrick H. Perrine is an immersive guide lighting the path towards entrepreneurial success.

This power-packed handbook propels you from dreaming to achieving with a carefully curated 100-step map. Dive into real-life entrepreneur stories, extract wisdom, and utilize actionable checklists. This book transcends theoretical guidelines, providing a mentorship experience designed to turn dreams into reality.

Ready to kindle your entrepreneurial spirit? "Ignite your Dream" is your step forward towards unlocking potential and achieving success in the exciting world of entrepreneurship.

Fail Fast, Recover Faster: Bouncing Back From Entrepreneurial Failure

Embrace failure and bounce back stronger with "Fail Fast, Recover Faster: Bouncing Back From Entrepreneurial Failure". It's your guidebook through the tumultuous journey of entrepreneurship, celebrating stumbles as stepping stones towards success.

Dive into compelling tales of triumphant entrepreneurs, learn how to pivot rapidly, manage fallout, and convert setbacks into launchpads. Discover strategies for repairing financial, relationship, and reputation damage, and see your failures as badges of resilience.

This transformative book readies you to rebound from failure swiftly, turning your setbacks into your next entrepreneurial triumph. With "Fail Fast, Recover Faster", you're poised to harness your own unicorn moment and turn failure into a launching pad for success.

Fueling the Fire: Nurturing Resilience and Preventing Burnout in Entrepreneurship

In "Fueling the Fire: Nurturing Resilience and Preventing Burnout in Entrepreneurship," seasoned entrepreneur Patrick H. Perrine guides you through the entrepreneurial journey, sharing practical strategies for maintaining resilience and passion.

Drawing from 20 years of startup experience, Perrine covers everything from ideation to acquisition. Discover how to build a support system, manage your time effectively, cultivate a positive work culture, and align your work with your values.

Whether you're an experienced entrepreneur or just beginning, "Fueling the Fire" is a must-read for maintaining balance and fulfillment in the dynamic world of entrepreneurship.

www.ingramcontent.com/pod-product-compliance
Lightning Source LLC
Chambersburg PA
CBHW070430290526
45791CB00005B/1907